The Tea Dragon Society

The Tea Dragon Society

WRITTEN & ILLUSTRATED BY

Katie O'Neill

LETTERED BY
Saida Temofonte

DESIGNED BY
Hilary Thompson

EDITED BY
Ari Yarwood

SCHOLASTIC INC.

ISBN 978-1-338-55293-5

Published by Scholastic Inc., 557 Broadway, New York, NY 10012, by
arrangement with Oni Press. SCHOLASTIC and associated logos are
trademarks and/or registered trademarks of Scholastic Inc.

12 11 10 9 8 7 6 5 4 3 2 1   19 20 21 22 23 24

Printed in the U.S.A.   40

First Scholastic printing, January 2019

CHAPTER ONE

Spring

Once upon a time, blacksmiths were as important as magicians.

They made tools for healers to cure the sick.

Swords for adventurers to slay monsters.

Shoes to shod the hooves of working animals.

The world was forged in iron... Once upon a time...

Greta! Are you listening?

Please pay attention, shaping hot swords is dangerous work even for those of us with goblin blood—as you well know.

Yes, Mama!

Sorry. I'll concentrate, I promise.

You must wait for the exact right color—do not let it get too hot or the sword will become weak.

And then...

...strike!!

Mama... do people use swords anymore? I thought they were just in stories.

Not so much, these days.

But they are beautiful objects, and they have a history.

But they don't... do anything.

Is this a way of telling me you are not interested in learning black-smithing?

No, no, I am! I want to learn from you... because you're the best at it!

I am very good—your father seems to have no trouble selling my work, even if people have no use for it.

I am happy you want to learn. You have a gift, Greta—you formed your pact with Brick when you were just six.

That's true...

EEEEEEEEEEEK!

SKREEEEEEK!

WEK!

Mama's gonna be mad about the meat, but that's okay...

No one deserves to starve.

You'll be fine. I think your pride got hurt more than anything, huh?

Greta! I saw blood on the doormat—are you all right?

I'm fine, Papa! The blood was from this little thing. She's doing better now.

I don't know who she belongs to, though. She seems like she wouldn't survive on her own.

Oh, I know her owner.

You do?

I sell him tea leaves from time to time—he only buys the very best.

He's a peculiar fellow, but I expect he'd be very grateful if you returned his dragon.

"He runs a tea shop just out of town.

"His name is Hesekiel."

Hello?

I think I have your—

Jasmine!

I thought you were gone...

...I hope you've learned never to run off in the marketplace.

Are you learning to take care of Tea Dragons, too?

Hesekiel just invited me to learn with him. Is that your own Tea Dragon?

It's okay, I'm not gonna take him. Let's be friends! My name's Greta.

16

CHAPTER TWO
Summer

I used this technique to make a teapot once... a man commissioned it for someone named Hesekiel. Papa told me that you have met him.

You know him, too?

We share mutual admiration for our crafts.

Actually, he invited me to come learn more about Tea Dragons...

...but that was over a month ago, and I've been too nervous to go! D'you think it's too late now?

"Hesekiel is not like humans and goblins. He will live for more than twice our lifespan.

"And Hesekiel himself is one who values patience in all things. I think he would barely notice your hesitation."

Hello. Please go through to the back, if you would like to meet the rest of the Tea Dragons.

I must work on filling these orders, but Erik will introduce you.

O—Okay!

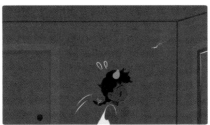

So, you're the one who's keen on these ratbags! A brave soul, to be sure.

They seem sweet.

Aye. They can be, if they know it'll get them something. Manipulative little buggers.

23

I'm Erik, by the way.

I'm Greta!

Anyone Hese trusts with his Dragon, I would trust with my life.

Let me show you how to get these rascals preening and purring.

You'll want a pair of these—if you rub them the wrong way, they're liable to take a nip at you.

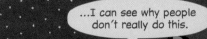

...I can see why people don't really do this.

Aye, it's a bit of a chore. At first I thought it was far too much fuss for a bit of leafy water.

Don't tell Hese I said that.

But I'll admit, the tea is worth it...

...not many people seem to think so, though. Harder and harder to find people interested in learning.

Hese is so happy that you're keen.

He doesn't want the knowledge to be lost.

Hello, Min! I was wondering where you'd been. Would you like something to eat?

nod

I just made leek and potato soup.

Hey, again.

I promise it turned out better than the last time I tried.

!

Careful, it's hot.

Thank you.

...What's up with her?

Goes by Minette, though we haven't been able to find out much else about her.

"She turned up in town one day and didn't seem to have anywhere to go.

Oh!

She forgot her spoon.

"Chamomile took such a liking to her that we offered her the tea house in the garden to nest up in.

I can take it to her!

"She's been here for a month or two."

You forgot this! I thought I'd bring it out to you.

Erik mentioned that you only came to town a few months ago...

...If you want, I could show you some of the secret places I like.

Never mind. Here's your spoon!

...I would like that.

Great! I'll meet you here tomorrow afternoon?

Wanna get a pastry?

...I don't have any money.

That's okay! I'll get two.

Thank you.

No worries. You've really never been here before? Have you ever left the tea shop?

No...

...I'm scared I'll forget the way back.

Forget?

When I was small, I was training to become a prophetess...

...I have the gift of future sight.

...At least, I used to.

"I was told I had great power, and a duty to use it.

"So every day I tried to see more and more, every future that could possibly exist.

"My mind was full to bursting. I burned out. To protect itself, my mind erased every memory I had.

"...Including the ones about me."

Even now, I forget stuff easily.

When you said, "Hey, again," yesterday, I had already forgotten that we had met before.

It's embarrassing. And scary.

Minette, if you ever get lost, I'll come and find you!

I promise!

Thank you, Greta.

31

CHAPTER THREE
Autumn

This is kinda relaxing when they aren't trying to bite your fingers off.

That's a good way to put it.

That should have been our slogan.

Slogan?

36

It won't be forgotten.

Brick, d'you think anyone else our age is learning blacksmithing?

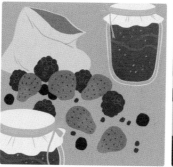

I appreciate the help, but I'm guessing it wasn't free.

Correct. I've been hoping someone would come and claim that bounty.

Don't like getting your hands dirty?

No, but I suspect you rather enjoy it.

I'm looking for someone with a big sword.

Guess that's me, all right.

If you can keep working magic like that, I'm up for a deal.

...This isn't what you signed up for.

I signed up to fight by your side.

To treat your wounds, to never abandon you.

You shouldn't have to give up exploring and adventure because of me. You loved that.

It was never the adventure that I loved.

Those were good days, adventuring about with a big idiot and his sword.

Yeah...

...but running the tea house turned into an adventure of its own.

C'mon, Chamomile. I'm sure it's this way.

I knew you'd get back on your own!

46

CHAPTER FOUR

Winter

Dear Mama and Papa,

I'm sorry for taking so long to write to you after I ran away from the monastery. I want to find out who am when I don't have my gift anymore, and what I want to do. I can only do this by myself, but I'm not alone. I have many good people looking after me, and will be home as soon as I'm ready.

Love,
Your Minette

It feels weird to write a letter to people I barely remember...

...I know that they love me, though.

Hopefully I can go home soon.

Say, Greta... would you help me make tea from *Chamomile's* flowers like Mr. Hesekiel did?

Sure! Haven't you tried it before?

No, not yet... I've been too nervous to.

Because of my memory...

...I was scared that even if I drank it, there'd be nothing to see.

But I'm ready to try.

I'll help for sure!

Memories don't just live inside you, Minette.

They live in all the people and objects you share your life with.

Chamomile, Erik, Hesekiel...

...and me, too!

You're right, Greta.

I lost so much and was scared of losing more. I didn't notice how many good memories I was making.

I'm thankful I met you.

Epilogue

I wanted to make something for you both.

As thanks for teaching me and Minette about Tea Dragons.

Greta... it's beautiful. Thank you.

Funny that, we actually have something for you too, Greta.

If you'd like to receive it.

This is Ginseng. Her owner sadly passed away, and there was no one left to care for her.

She needs a caretaker... would you like to be one, Greta?

She's so sad...

Tea Dragons get very attached to their companions.

It may take her a while to bond with you...

...and even then, she will still require diligent care and attention.

You don't have to take on the responsibility, Greta.

I want to.

I want to make good memories with all of you. And with Ginseng, too.

Now that we each have a Tea Dragon, I reckon we could call ourselves a society again. What d'you think?

I think that would be wonderful.

Welcome to the ancient and noble art of Tea Dragon husbandry...

Raising Tea Dragons is a highly rewarding and satisfying practice, though it requires a great deal of time and dedication. This book merely scratches the surface of knowledge that has been handed down across thousands of years, from one owner to another. It is advised that you read all of the content before deciding whether to raise a Tea Dragon or not, as it is a large commitment and not to be made lightly. For those who do choose this path, you will find a loving and loyal companion your whole life long.

ABOUT TEA DRAGONS

Tea Dragons are a small, highly domesticated breed of dragon that grow tea leaves out of their horns and antlers. The type of tea depends on the Dragon, and although mixed-tea varieties are possible, it is generally considered better practice to grow pure strains of tea and then mix as desired later. The Dragons retain the haughtiness and pride of their much larger ancestors; however, they lack any survival capabilities whatsoever. This makes them have high expectations of care and attention, and they become very nervous and worried if they are separated from their primary caregiver.

They have very specific requirements for grooming and care, such as daily brushing and rubbing with oils. Most Tea Dragons have short fur, though for some it is so short as to be more like a soft leather. They enjoy luxurious scented oils from almonds, olives and flowers, and the grooming process is a chance for the owner to bond with them. It can take a while to figure out the exact preferred brushing and polishing methods of each Dragon, so to begin with leather gloves is advised to protect from angry nips.

The tea leaves grown from their horns and antlers produce a very high quality tea that, when brewed correctly, has magical properties. Through their close bond and constant companionship, Tea Dragons naturally absorb and remember the various experiences they share with their owners. They are watchful creatures, and store these memories in their magical horns. The images are then imbued into the tea leaves, and so when brewed provide a taste of what was experienced. In this way they are able to give back to their owners for all the diligent and careful care they receive.

Tea Dragons are a very long-lived species, and well cared-for Dragons can live for over a thousand years. Sadly, this means they will outlive a number of owners. Due to their close bond, when an owner passes away, the dragon will shed its tea leaves in mourning and no longer produce any leaves that contain memories of that person. Therefore if others wish to preserve the memories, they will need to be careful to collect those fallen leaves. It takes a while—usually several years—before they begin to bond with a new caregiver. Once they trust a new owner, however, their adoration and dependence will be as strong as ever.

In this way, passing Tea Dragons from one owner to the next, the tradition has been kept alive for thousands of years across many generations. It is hoped that people such as yourself, reader, will be part of keeping this chain going into the future, bringing the joy of Tea Dragons to new ages.

TEA DRAGON SOCIETIES

Due to the highly specialised nature of raising Tea Dragons, many groups have formed throughout the world to exchange knowledge, skills and advice. Long-time owners of Tea Dragons joke that these are "support groups." As Tea Dragons are a lifelong commitment, these societies don't always meet very often—twice a year is common, in summer and winter. The meetings are always accompanied by lots of fresh fruit, cheese and baked goods, and of course cups of tea. It is a good chance for Tea Dragons to socialise with others of their kind—they usually are too haughty to play or groom one another, but it reminds them that they are in fact dragons and not very small people.

Friendships formed at these meetings prove to be very strong—even if members lose touch with one another for several years or even decades, when they finally meet it is as if no time has passed. Perhaps this is because Tea Dragons remind one of how a decade is not very much time at all when you live for centuries. Owners of Tea Dragons often report that they felt themselves becoming more relaxed and peaceful after obtaining their Dragon, despite the rigorousness of the care required for them.

These societies are also an excellent way of comparing and learning from different Dragon care methods from many different cultures. Tea Dragons are found throughout the world in many different varieties depending on the endemic tea species, and each region has its own ways of grooming, feeding and collecting Tea Dragon leaves. Owners who have difficulties with their Dragon may find a method developed in a different country works better for them.

TEA DRAGON DAILY LIFE

Tea Dragons eat a staple diet of root vegetables, insects and fruit. They can be fed herbs and vegetables flavoured with spices in order to enhance and accent the flavour of their tea. Each Tea Dragon has a different eating schedule, which can only be discovered through trial and error. They must be fed at exactly the right time, or they will be affronted and refuse to eat at all that day.

Some Tea Dragon owners spoil their Dragon with sugary snacks. This is not advised, as it puts the Dragons into a very bad mood. For Tea Dragon treats, extra-ripe fruits and baked vegetables such as pumpkin or squash are the best choice. It should be noted that Tea Dragons are lactose intolerant.

Tea Dragons do not require play; they require entertainment. Tea Dragons are proud and will not actively engage themselves in activities unless tricked into it. The good news is that Tea Dragons are immensely curious and nosy, and following their owner around as they perform daily tasks such as cooking, cleaning or going to the market is usually sufficiently entertaining. For most owners, it becomes hard to imagine going about everyday life without a sniffling inquisitive nose poking into their business.

TEA DRAGON LEAVES

One of the most remarkable properties of Tea Dragon tea leaves is that they store the memories and experiences the Tea Dragon shares with the owner. When stored and brewed correctly, they can bring these memories back to life through a mixture of taste, smell and vision created by drinking the tea. Little is known about why these memories began to be imbued into the tea leaves by the Dragons, but it only occurs when the bond between Dragon and owner is strong. Only experiences between the two are kept, nothing that the Dragon would have experienced on their own.

In order to preserve the memories at full strength, the leaves must be harvested at full bloom, collected carefully, dried and stored. Brewing fresh tea leaves directly will still create an effect, but it will not be as strong or pronounced as the dried tea. To brew the tea, it is preferred to use a cast iron tea pot to infuse minerals into the water. Heat the water to just before boiling point—it is important not to let it scald the leaves or the memories will appear foggy and unclear. It should be allowed to steep for 4-5 minutes, then drunk immediately.

Leaves from two different Dragons that share a strong connection can be brewed together to unify their shared experiences with their owners. This is a rare occurrence, as it takes a long time for Tea Dragons to bond to one another—much longer than to a new owner. However they will eventually settle into an easy grace with each other, as long as they both feel they are receiving adequate attention from their respective caregivers.

When drinking someone else's tea, you will be able to sense and see the memories stored in the leaves; however, the effect is far stronger for whomever the Dragon is primarily bonded with. For an outsider it will be like reading or watching a story—for the owner, it will feel like living that day again.

Jasmine Tea Dragon

AVERAGE LENGTH: 50 cm

AVERAGE WEIGHT: 5 kg

TEA BREWED BY: Leaves

CARE NOTES: Toenails grow very fast and require frequent trimming. Makes guttural screech noises when scared or displeased.

Jasmine Tea Dragons have a great deal of poise and elegance, and are probably the most self-conscious out of all the Dragons. They are watchful and intelligent, though this doesn't translate to any extra survival capability. With keen beady eyes, they quickly understand and interpret what their owners are doing during their daily routine, which makes it much easier to interfere and be a pest.

Rooibos Tea Dragon

AVERAGE LENGTH: 35 cm

AVERAGE WEIGHT: 10 kg

TEA BREWED BY: Leaves, dried flowers

CARE NOTES: Enjoys rough and tumble sparring, but the Dragon must always be allowed to win or they'll stop wanting to play.

Rooibos Tea Dragons are stout and active little creatures, and are happy to follow their owner on any adventure. Tea Dragons don't normally enjoy play activities, but Rooibos are the exception. Unfortunately, they don't realise that other Dragons don't share this enthusiasm, and will gently butt their heads against their chosen playmate for hours, trying to raise a response.

Chamomile Tea Dragon

AVERAGE LENGTH: 40 cm

AVERAGE WEIGHT: 8 kg

TEA BREWED BY: Dried flowers

CARE NOTES: Unbelievably relaxed and sleepy, owners may need to wake them up to remind them to eat.

Chamomile Tea Dragons are probably the easiest variety for new owners to care for, as they are so relaxed and easygoing that it is very hard to bother them. They do have specific dietary preferences, but rather than getting upset, they will simply not bother eating, which can make it difficult to know what exactly they want. They sleep for around 18 hours a day.

Ginseng Tea Dragon

AVERAGE LENGTH: 30 cm

AVERAGE WEIGHT: 10 kg

TEA BREWED BY: Leaves and berries

CARE NOTES: Curious and with a keen sense of smell, they are liable to follow a scent for hours and get lost.

Ginseng Tea Dragons have one of the strongest bonds with their owners, and constantly look for ways to be praised by them. One of their favourite methods is to find and bring foods they know their owner likes. Unfortunately, they have no concept of property ownership, so this often ends with their owner apologising to whoever's goods they have stolen.

Earl Grey Tea Dragon

AVERAGE LENGTH: 55 cm

AVERAGE WEIGHT: 10 kg

TEA BREWED BY: Leaves & bergamot oil

CARE NOTES: Only grows one bergamot on its horns each year, and without the oil from this, the tea will have no magical property.

Earl Grey Tea Dragons are affectionately referred to by enthusiasts as "Little Grandpas." They have a very dignified and habitual manner, and require strict accordance to daily schedules. They are thoughtful and quiet, and prefer to watch and observe rather than poke their nose in their owner's business. That said, if they think no one is watching, they can be caught in all manner of silly poses.

Hibiscus Tea Dragon

AVERAGE LENGTH: 40 cm

AVERAGE WEIGHT: 12 kg

TEA BREWED BY: Flowers

CARE NOTES: Prefers a warm climate with high humidity, and becomes sluggish at cold temperatures.

Hibiscus Tea Dragons are second only to Chamomile Dragons in terms of easygoing nature. They love to eat, and especially to share food with their owners, and have more adventurous tastebuds than most other Dragons. They are also extremely sociable, and owners of Hibiscus Dragons often report that they find themselves more compelled to try new foods and talk to new people.

Ginger Tea Dragon

AVERAGE LENGTH: 40 cm

AVERAGE WEIGHT: 8 kg

TEA BREWED BY: Leaves & horn extract

CARE NOTES: The horn is similar in texture and density to a root, and a tiny shaving will give the tea its ginger taste.

Ginger Tea Dragons are cautious and sensitive, and very attuned to moods and emotions. They are less proud than other Dragons but often shy, and will openly display affection for their owner but only in private. It is said that they can sense illness in people, and will try to alert those around them if they think someone is unwell and needs attention.

Peppermint Tea Dragon

AVERAGE LENGTH: 30 cm

AVERAGE WEIGHT: 5 kg

TEA BREWED BY: Leaves

CARE NOTES: Hates to be left alone, and will begin crying immediately if it thinks it has been abandoned.

Peppermint Tea Dragons are cheerful and friendly, but extremely needy. Their feelings are hurt easily by lack of attention. They don't like to feel second-place to anyone, and need constant assurance and affection. They are, however, excellent Tea Dragons for owners with families, as they love young children and are extremely patient with them.

Katie O'Neill is an illustrator & graphic novelist from New Zealand.

She is the author of *Princess Princess Ever After*, *The Tea Dragon Society*, and *Aquicorn Cove*, all from Oni Press. She mostly makes gentle fantasy stories for younger readers, and is very interested in tea, creatures, things that grow, and the magic of everyday life.

ALSO FROM KATIE O'NEILL

PRINCESS PRINCESS EVER AFTER

Join Sadie and Amira, two very different princesses with very different strengths, on their journey to figure out what "happily ever after" really means—and how they can find it with each other.

AQUICORN COVE

Unable to rely on the adults in her storm-ravaged seaside town, a young girl must protect a colony of magical seahorse-like creatures she discovers in the coral reef.

THE TEA DRAGON SOCIETY CARD GAME

Create a bond between yourself and your Tea Dragon in this easy-to-learn card game from Oni Games and Renegade Games!

LOOK FOR MORE TEA DRAGON ADVENTURES IN...

The Tea Dragon Festival
COMING FALL 2019!

CHECK OUT TEADRAGONSOCIETY.COM FOR UPDATES & MORE ABOUT TEA DRAGONS!